PHOTOGRAPHER UNKNOWN
DUET, 1959

*The files of UPI are full of feline newsmakers. At one point, pictures of cats ran two-to-one
against pictures of children, and five-to-one against pictures of dogs.*

# FUNNY
# CATS

EDITED BY
## J. C. SUARÈS

TEXT BY
### JANE MARTIN

## WELCOME ENTERPRISES, INC.
### NEW YORK

First Published 1995 by Welcome Enterprises, Inc.
588 Broadway, New York, NY 10012

Distributed by Stewart, Tabori & Chang
a division of U.S. Media Holdings, Inc.
115 West 18th Street, New York, NY 10011
Distributed in Canada by General Publishing Co., Ltd.
30 Lesmill Road, Don Mills, Ontario, Canada M3B 2T6
Distributed in the U.K. by Hi Marketing
38 Carver Road, London SE24 9LT, United Kingdom
Distributed in Australia by Peribo Pty Ltd.
58 Beaumont Road, Mount Kuring-gai NSW 2080, Australia
Distributed in New Zealand by Tandem Press
2 Rugby Road, Auckland 10, New Zealand

The publishers gratefully acknowledge the permission of the following to
reprint the copyrighted material in this book:

Excerpts on pp. 12, 46: P.G. Wodehouse, "The Story of Webster,"
permission given by A.P. Watt on behalf of the Trustees of the
Wodehouse Estate.

Excerpt on p. 44: Translated by Patrick and Justina Gregory, in The
Fables of Aesop, selected and illustrated by David Levine, © 1975,
David Levine.

Excerpt on p. 56 from "How the Cat Became," in How the Whale
Became and Other Stories, by Ted Hughes, © Ted Hughes, 1963,
Faber and Faber Ltd., publishers.

Excerpt on p. 78 from "the song of mehitabel" from archy and
mehitabel, by Don Marquis, © 1927 by Doubleday, a division of
Bantam Doubleday Dell Publishing Group, Inc., Reprinted by
permission of the publisher.

Library of Congress Card Catalog Number: 95-060047
ISBN 0-941807-11-8 (previously ISBN 1-55670-411-9)

Printed and bound in Spain. D.L. TO: 81-1999
10 9 8 7 6

TITLE PAGE: ELLIOTT ERWITT
ROME, ITALY, 1959

JOYCE RAVID
BATTY, WRITER'S BLOCK, 1992

S HE WAS YELLOW WITH WHITE SOCKS, AND A LITTLE ON THE HEAVY SIDE PERHAPS, BUT SHE SEEMED LIKE A PERFECTLY NORMAL CAT WHEN SHE ARRIVED TO SPEND TWO WEEKS WITH ME WHILE HER OWNER WAS ON A TRIP TO IRELAND. I NEVER ASKED WHY HER NAME WAS BANSHEE (ACCORDING TO IRISH FOLKLORE, A FEMALE SPIRIT BELIEVED TO WAIT OUTSIDE A HOUSE AS A WARNING THAT SOMEONE IN THE HOUSE WILL SOON DIE). IT NEVER OCCURRED TO ME TO ASK. BUT IT WASN'T LONG BEFORE IT BECAME CLEAR HOW SHE GOT HER NAME: BANSHEE WAS SIMPLY OUT OF HER DAMNED MIND. 🐾 WHERE MOST CATS ARE RECLUSIVE AND CAUTIOUS, BANSHEE WAS A LOOSE CANNON; AS FAST AS A SHOOTING STAR AND WITH THE AUDACITY OF A KAMIKAZE PILOT. PLANTS, PEOPLE, FURNITURE, DRAPES, AND OTHER PETS DIDN'T STAND A CHANCE IN HER WAY. 🐾 THE FIRST TIME I OPENED THE REFRIGERATOR, BANSHEE APPEARED OUT OF NOWHERE, PULLED OUT PACKAGES OF COLD CUTS AND CHEESES, AND STARTED CHEWING ON THEM WITH A LOUD GROWL. WHEN A BIRD APPEARED OUTSIDE, SHE TRIED TO TEAR THE CURTAINS DOWN WITH HER CLAWS. I DECIDED THIS WAS A TACTIC MEANT TO PROTEST THE BIRD'S ABILITY TO FLY, SINCE IT COULDN'T POSSIBLY HAVE BEEN A WAY TO GET AT THE BIRD. IF ANOTHER CAT WAS FAST

ASLEEP IN ONE OF THE BASKETS I HAD AROUND THE HOUSE, BANSHEE WOULD INVARIABLY PUNCH THE BASKET SO HARD THAT THE SLEEPING CAT WOULD BE HURTLED INTO THE AIR—NOT BECAUSE BANSHEE WANTED THE BASKET FOR HERSELF, MIND YOU, BUT BECAUSE SHE SIMPLY GOT A KICK OUT OF IT. 🐾 EVERY MORNING, BANSHEE WAITED PATIENTLY FOR HER TURN AT THE BATHROOM. SHE USED THE TOILET LIKE EVERYBODY ELSE AND DRANK FROM THE FAUCET. IF THE BATHTUB WAS FULL, SHE'D RUN AROUND IT IN A STATE OF HYSTERIA AS IF SHE HAD LOST SOMETHING. SHE'D REACH FOR IMAGINARY CREATURES AT THE BOTTOM, WHICH ONCE CAUSED HER TO FALL IN. LANDING IN A FULL BATHTUB WOULD BE A HUMILIATING EXPERIENCE FOR MOST CATS. BANSHEE, ON THE CONTRARY, WAS INVIGORATED. 🐾 ON CHRISTMAS EVE SHE CLIMBED DEEP INTO OUR TWELVE-FOOT CHRISTMAS TREE AND GOT SO CAUGHT UP IN THE BRANCHES THAT SHE HAD NO WAY OF GETTING OUT. REALIZING SHE WAS STUCK, SHE LET OUT A SERIES OF BLOODCURDLING HOWLS. I WANTED TO SHOOT HER THAT NIGHT, BUT SHE WAS TOO ENTERTAINING. IN THE END, I ACTUALLY MISSED HER. DESPITE THE BROKEN VASES, DEAD PLANTS, TERRIFIED GUESTS, AND TORN WALLPAPER AND CURTAINS, I WAS SORRY TO SEE HER GO.—*J.C. SUARÈS*

MIKE NELSON
SOCKS, LITTLE ROCK,
ARKANSAS, 1992

*This was taken outside the Governor's mansion during the campaign, sometime just before Thanksgiving. We had to stake out the mansion all day—get there before dawn. Since there was a chance he would be president, you had to treat him like the president. A few days earlier there had been a picture of Socks being held up by a television guy, which made Chelsea very upset. So Clinton had issued official instructions that the press should not touch the cat. We thought that was kind of a joke, and made up press passes with "no touch" signs.*

*Normally Clinton would jog after sunrise and we'd chase after him, but this morning he didn't run. As the morning progressed, we had to give the wire services something. When Socks came out, one photographer went after him, then a second, then a third—Reuters, UPI, AP, television. Once they started going it became a stampede. I decided to shoot the scene instead of the cat.*

*The picture went everywhere. Clinton saw it when he went to Washington the next day. He was incensed. Not only had we not left the cat alone, but we were cornering it. And it looks like one of us was luring Socks with catnip, though it wasn't true. But when that photographer's wire service saw the picture he was pulled out and sent back to Washington. Then everybody started getting into the scene. The tv guys got into it, and wanted to interview us. Instead I escaped to Memphis. The picture spawned a lot of cartoons about Socks being protected by the Secret Service, and the whole situation was completely blown out of proportion. But there's no way you could set up this picture.*

KRITINA LEE KNIEF
CAT POSING, NEW YORK, 1992

*This is Alfie, who arrived on my doorstep nine years ago. I'd just lost a cat and my friends found her. They asked me if I could just watch her overnight. Of course that stretched out to a little longer. I can always count on her to stay in one place.*

PHOTOGRAPHER UNKNOWN
CAT'S-EYE VIEW, C. 1945

*So many gag photos were sent over the wire to newspapers across the country that a cat's most unnatural behavior became perfectly unsurprising. Still, no one will ever know what really sent this large American Shorthair to the viewfinder of the Speed Graphic, or whether—a moment later—the tripod stayed up.*

"What I've got against cats," said a Lemon Sour, speaking feelingly,

as one brooding on a private grievance, "is their unreliability.

They lack candor and are not square shooters. You get your cat and you

call him Thomas or George, as the case may be. So far, so good.

Then one morning you wake up and find six kittens in the hat box and

you have to re-open the whole matter...."

**P.G. WODEHOUSE**
**The Story of Webster**

PHOTOGRAPHER UNKNOWN
MAURICE CHEVALIER AND CAT, C. 1925

*The young French crooner and his slightly cross-eyed partner sport twin straw boaters
for this portrait of two dandies.*

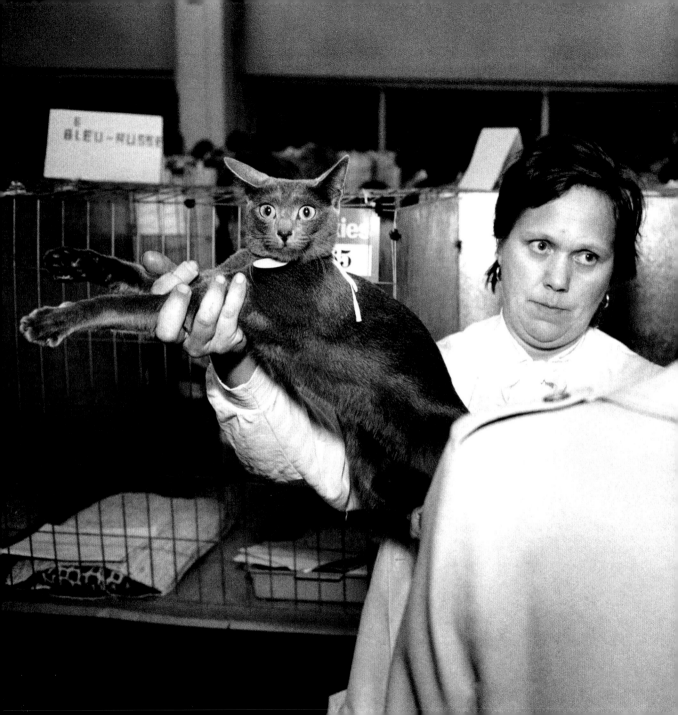

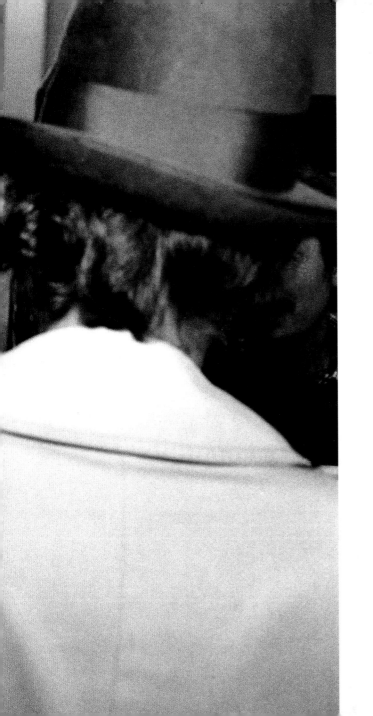

RICHARD KALVAR
PARIS, 1985

*"O my Enemy and Wife of my Enemy and Mother of my Enemy,"*

*said the Cat, "it is I: for you have spoken three words in my praise,*

*and now I can drink the warm white milk three times a day for always*

*and always and always. But still I am the Cat who walks by himself,*

*and all places are alike to me." Then the Woman laughed*

*and set the Cat a bowl of warm white milk and said, "O Cat, you are*

*as clever as a man, but remember that your bargain was not made*

*with the Man or the Dog, and I do not know what they will do when*

*they come home." "What is that to me?" said the Cat. "If I have*

*my place in the Cave by the fire and my warm white milk three times*

*a day. I do not care what the Man or the Dog can do."*

...............................................

**RUDYARD KIPLING**
**The Cat Who Walked by Himself**

PHOTOGRAPHER UNKNOWN
MILKTIME, C. 1940

*A farmer's tabby gets his customary treat during a milking—one of the countless cat
photographs sent over the wire during the heyday of small-town Americana scenes.*

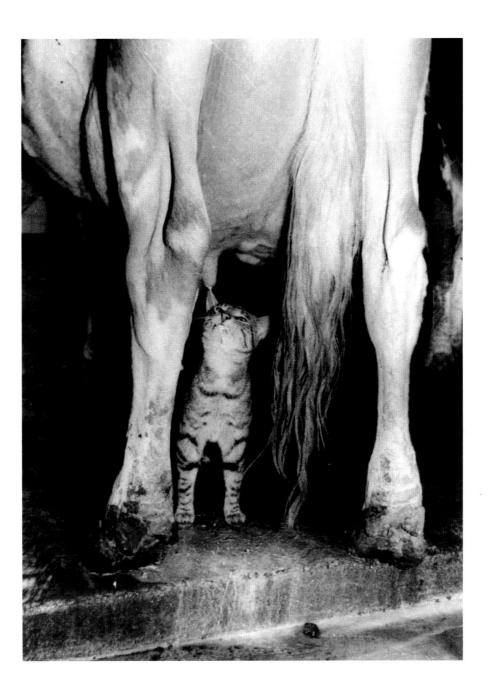

DAVID McENERY
HAT CAT, 1992

*There's a pet store in Santa Monica that lends me kittens for a few days.*
*This was one of the loaners.*

KRITINA LEE KNIEF
KITTEN IN HAT BOX, 1991

*This was taken in Boston for my children's book,* Alphabet Cats. *The little guy's name is Muddy Waters. His breeder, who's known for her Persians, names all her cats after musicians. We put fifteen kittens and cats in this set, and they had a great romp, scattering the boxes and crushing the hats. It may have been work to us, but it was a playground to them.*

L A R S  P E T E R  R O O S
W E S T  A F R I C A ,  1 9 8 6

*I had a good friend involved in a health project there, and when I stayed in her house, her cat
followed me everywhere. I'd sit down to eat my breakfast and there he'd be.*

H A R V E Y  S T E I N
C O N E Y  I S L A N D ,  1 9 7 3

*I used to go to Coney Island a lot—usually to take pictures of the people. But I passed an
open-air bar and this cat was sitting on the stool, stealing the scene.*

DAVID MCENERY
CAT IN SHADES, 1993

*This is the male kitten of a friend's cat's litter.*
*He was the most outgoing of all of them, a real showcat.*

DAVID McENERY
CATNAP I, 1979

*That is a genuine English deck chair and those are my wife, Pat McEnery's, feet.*
*The picture was taken on our patio soon after I came to America. The kitten was borrowed.*

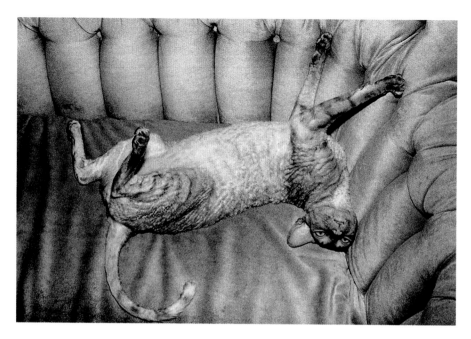

R O B I N   S C H W A R T Z
N O A H ,   1 9 9 3

*That's my boy, a Cornish Rex, at five. He's extremely attached and personable.*
*The thing about Rexes is that they act like dogs. People say that I have a dog that acts like a cat*
*and cats that act like dogs. Noah stands at the top of the shower doors when I take a shower and*
*sleeps in the baby bed when I work. Here he has the night crazies and is just trying to be funny.*


K A R L   B A D E N
C A T   S H O W ,   B O X B O R O U G H ,   M A S S A C H U S E T T S ,   1 9 9 3

*I often find the cages as interesting as the cats.*


O V E R L E A F :   P H O T O G R A P H E R   U N K N O W N
C A T S I T T I N G ,   c .   1 9 6 0

*Unlikely as the scene may seem, cats have been known to strike a maternal bond with many a*
*potential prey, such as this drowsy tabby has with the small dove.*

*For having done duty and received blessing he begins to consider himself.*

*For this he performs in ten degrees.*

*For first he looks upon his fore-paws to see if they are clean.*

*For secondly he kicks up behind to clear away there.*

*For thirdly he works it upon stretch with the fore-paws extended.*

*For fourthly he sharpens his paws by wood.*

*For fifthly he washes himself.*

*For sixthly he rolls upon wash.*

*For seventhly he fleas himself, that he may not be interrupted upon the beat.*

*For eighthly he rubs himself against a post.*

*For ninthly he looks up for his instructions.*

*For tenthly he goes in quest for food.*

**CHRISTOPHER SMART**
**Jubilate Agno**

WALTER CHANDOHA
OH, THAT FEELS GOOD, 1955

*When we lived on Long Island I got my first cat, Loco—a very resourceful fellow.*
*He liked to sharpen his claws on the bark, as cats do. Then, always wanting to get more*
*for his money, he'd turn around to scratch his back.*

STUDIO LEMAIRE
A TOAST, 1994

KRITINA LEE KNIEF
SINBAD AND ALFIE, 1985

*These are my cats in Weehawken, New Jersey,
where I lived then. I had just recently taken in Alfie,
the orphan kitten. Sinbad, who was usually not
very cordial to other cats, just fell in love with Alfie.
He'd let her do anything to him.*

OVERLEAF: TERRY deROY GRUBER
WHOOPSIE AND POOPSIE,
NEW YORK, 1979

*These are the cats of the Offset Printing Company,
on Broome Street in Soho. They have a lot of
Russian Blue blood. I'd heard a lot about them, but
every time I went to take their picture they were out.
The sixth time I showed up, they were both in. As soon
as I made the shot they took off again. Some of the
customers call them the Bureaucats, since they do
nothing around there but hold up the operation.*

*A Cat, hearing that there were some sick Birds in the neighborhood, got himself up as a doctor and set off to pay a house call. When he arrived at their home he called out to ask how the occupants were getting on. "Very well, thank you," came the reply, "if only you would go away."*

**AESOP**
***The Cat and the Birds***

JAN RIETZ
CAT ON BIRDHOUSE, 1987

*This was taken when my cat Millie was already ten years old. Even though Millie is a feminine name, he was a very male cat. He was a nice cat too, and an optimist—he was sure that the birds would fly right into his mouth as they headed for the birdhouse.*

*Webster was very large and very black and very composed.*

*He conveyed the impression of being a cat of deep reserves.*

*Descendant of a long line of ecclesiastical ancestors who had conducted*

*their decorous courtships beneath the show of cathedrals*

*and on the back walls of the bishops' palaces, he had that exquisite poise*

*which one sees in high dignitaries of the Church.*

.............................................................

**P.G. WODEHOUSE**
**The Story of Webster**

TERRY deROY GRUBER
PARAMUS, NEW JERSEY, 1979

*This seemed to me like the perfect combination. The judge holding Stanley, an Oriental*
*Shorthair, said, "It's tough modeling all day and traveling all over the country.*
*But Stanley here knows what he's doing."*

ROBIN SCHWARTZ
BALOO, NEW YORK, 1993

*Baloo was at the Madison Square Garden Cat Show in March. She's a Norwegian Forest Cat. She was just hanging out on the chair, very laid back. I think it's remarkable for a cat to act that way at a cat show. I'd be a wreck if I were a cat at a cat show.*

DAVID MCENERY
LOST NOTE, 1992

*That's Lovejoy, our own kitten. He's a very curious cat.*
*You just leave him alone and let him go.*

WALTER CHANDOHA
GREENWICH VILLAGE, NEW YORK, 1954

*My friend Mabel Schezleri was the cat columnist for the old World Telegram.*
*Her nom de plume was Henrietta Hitchcock. One day we were just fooling around and her cat*
*got onto the kitchen table and sat in the bowl.*


OVERLEAF: WALTER CHANDOHA
HERE'S LOOKING AT YOU, NEW YORK, 1956

*This was taken in a New York apartment. The kitten, a Siamese,*
*just rushed up to the mirror and started staring.*

Cat was a real oddity. The others didn't know what to make of him
at all. He lived in a hollow tree in the wood. Every night, when the
rest of the creatures were sound asleep, he retired to the depths of his
tree—then such sounds, such screechings, yowlings, wailings!
The bats that slept upside-down all day long in the hollows of the tree
branches awoke with a start and fled with their wing-tips stuffed into
their ears. It seemed to them that Cat was having the worst nightmares
ever—ten at a time! But no. Cat was tuning his violin.

..............................................

**TED HUGHES**
**How the Cat Became**

ROBIN SCHWARTZ
SAFRAM SPHYNX KITTENS, YORKTOWN HEIGHTS,
NEW YORK, 1993

*I went to Safram, Sandra Adler's cattery, to see her new litter. They were very young, and very
unkitten-like. Rumpelstiltskin is the one sitting up. The Sphynx is a rare breed: there are
less than six hundred in the world, though they've been around for a hundred years. According to
the breed's historians, they're descended from a feral cat on the streets of Toronto, or from a
Minnesota barn cat. They used to just appear as a mutant gene in litters, but now they're bred
very carefully. As kittens, they feel like warm suede. Sandra says that the word 'alien'
seems more appropriate than cat.*

The Cat only grinned when it saw Alice. It looked good-natured, she thought: still it had very long claws and a good many teeth, so she felt that it ought to be treated with respect. "Cheshire Puss," she began, rather timidly, as she did not at all know whether it would like the name: however, it only grinned a little wider. "Come, it's pleased so far," thought Alice, and she went on. "Would you tell me, please, which way I ought to go from here?"

"That depends a good deal on where you want to go," said the Cat.

"I don't much care where——" said Alice.

"Then it doesn't matter which way you go," said the Cat.

"——so long as I get somewhere," Alice added as an explanation.

"Oh, you're sure to do that," said the Cat, "if only you walk long enough."

Alice felt that this could not be denied, so she tried another question.

"What sort of people live around here?"

"In that direction," the Cat said, waving its right paw round, "lives a Hatter and in that direction," waving the other paw, "lives a March Hare. Visit either you like: they're both mad."

"But I don't want to go among mad people," Alice remarked.

"Oh, you can't help that," said the Cat. "We're all mad here. I'm mad. You're mad."

"How do you know I'm mad?" said Alice.

"You must be," said the Cat, "or you wouldn't be here."

LEWIS CARROLL
*Alice's Adventures in Wonderland*

WALTER CHANDOHA
CHESHIRE CAT, 1972

*I'm fascinated by the idea of a grinning cat. This was Smiley, one of our cats,
and his expression is as close to the Cheshire cat as I've come.*

*A typesetter at this firm, which was called Zinn's and was in midtown, told me that Zinn the cat was great to have around the office, since she was a real talker, and it was nice to have someone to make conversation with when you just worked with printed words all day.*

KARL BADEN
CAT SHOW, FRAMINGHAM, MASSACHUSETTS, 1991

*The show was taking place in a high school gym, which seemed like a very noisy atmosphere. What interested me is that someone put a bed in the cage that's about three times as fancy as the one I sleep in, though it's a little smaller, of course.*

TERRY deROY GRUBER
GROCERY STORE CAT,
NEW YORK, 1979

*The stock boy told me that he was over on Aisle B
with the household supplies, just stamping prices.
He reached up to a shelf and started stocking and whap!
The little monster nailed him.*

DAVID MCENERY
CATNAP II, 1992

*My wife, Pat, made the hammock. She's a great*
*hammock maker. The kitten thought so too.*
*They don't have hammocks at the pet store.*


OVERLEAF: WALTER CHANDOHA
TICKLING THE IVORIES, 1957

*I guess the kitten liked the sound of the keys.*

KRITINA LEE KNIEF
CAT IN LEATHER JACKET, NEW YORK, 1992

*His name is Buddy Rodriguez. He's a friend's kitten, bought from someone
at a flea market holding a "kittens for sale" sign. He was perfect—really into cuddling.
He would fall asleep all the time. We had to keep him awake.*

OVERLEAF: LARS PETER ROOS
BURMA KATTER, STOCKHOLM, 1988

*My friend Peter put his Burmese cats, Lotus and Julia, on the double doors because he knew they
liked to sit there. They were sisters from the same litter, and the real owners of Peter's apartment.*

JIM MCLAGAN
BATHTIME, 1982

*ARIES (March 21–April 20)*

*The original cat on a hot tin roof, most active and ambitious of them
all. From clean laundry to flower beds, he makes a (hollow) impression
everywhere. Fond of wandering, and when at home liable to create his
own obstacle course with no inhibitions about broken ornaments.*

*Fond of fighting, impetuous at loving.*

*Best Owners (only owners able to survive him): Sagittarius, Leo.*

.........................................................

**ANN CURRAH**
**The Cat Horoscope**

PHOTOGRAPHER UNKNOWN
AUDREY HEPBURN AND THE CAT CALLED CAT, 1961

*Orangey, a 14-pound prima donna, is a legend in the small world of feline acting.
His Patsy-award winning performance in* Breakfast at Tiffany's *required all the efforts of his
trainer, Frank Inn, including guard dogs at the exits so Orangey would stick around.
It was his second Patsy, the first gleaned from his work in the 1952 feature* Rhubarb, *which
also earned him the title, "The World's Meanest Cat."*

do you think that i would change

my present freedom to range

for a castle or moated grange

wotthehell wotthehell

cage me and i d go frantic

my life is so romantic

capricious and corybantic

and i m toujours gai toujours gai

**DON MARQUIS**
*the song of mehitabel*

GUY LE QUERREC
VILLE JUIF, 1975

*Taken in a suburb near Paris.*

do you think that i would change

my present freedom to range

for a castle or moated grange

wotthehell wotthehell

cage me and i d go frantic

my life is so romantic

capricious and corybantic

and i m toujours gai toujours gai

...............................................

**DON MARQUIS**
*the song of mehitabel*

GUY LE QUERREC
VILLE JUIF, 1975

*Taken in a suburb near Paris.*

*34-5: Courtesy American Stock/Archive Photos*

*11, 13, 17: Courtesy Archive Photos*

*33, 63: © Karl Baden/ Courtesy Robert Mann Gallery New York,*
*        and Howard Yezerski Gallery, Boston*

*1: Courtesy the Bettmann Archive*

*37, 53, 54-5, 59, 68-9: © Walter Chandoha*

*77: Courtesy Culver Pictures*

*12: Walt Disney Studios/Courtesy Archive Photos*

*Title page: © Elliott Erwitt/Magnum Photos*

*22-3: Courtesy Express Newspapers/Archive Photos*

*28-9, 42-3, 47, 60-1, 64-5: © Terry deRoy Gruber*

*14-5: © Richard Kalvar/Magnum Photos*

*10, 19, 40-1, 71: © Kritina Lee Knief*

*79: © Guy le Querrec/Magnum Photos*

*75: © Jim McLagan/Argus Newspapers, South Africa*

*18, 26-7, 31, 50-1, 66-7: © David McEnery*

*8-9: © Mike Nelson/Agence France Presse*

*21: © Nick Nichols/Magnum Photos*

*5: © Joyce Ravid*

*45: © Jan Rietz/Tiofoto AB*

*24, 72-3: © Lars Peter Roos/Tiofoto AB*

*32, 49, 57: © Robin Schwartz*

*25: © Harvey Stein*

*39: © Studio Lemaire/Art Unlimited, Amsterdam*